ITALY

LETTERS FROM AROUND THE WORLD

Fiona Tankard

Photographs by Sue Cunningham

CHERRYTREE BOOKS

LETTERS FROM AROUND THE WORLD

Titles in this series

BANGLADESH · BRAZIL · CHINA · FRANCE · INDIA · ITALY · JAMAICA · JAPAN · KENYA · SPAIN

A Cherrytree Book

Conceived and produced by

Nutshell MEDIA

Intergen House
65-67 Western Road
Hove BN3 2JQ, UK
www.nutshellmedialtd.co.uk

First published by
Evans Brothers Ltd
2A Portman Mansions
Chiltern Street
London W1U 6NR

VISIT OUR WEBSITE
Evans
www.evansbooks.co.uk

Reprinted 2006
Editor: Katie Orchard
Designer: Tim Mayer
Map artwork: Encompass Graphics Ltd
All other artwork: Tim Mayer
Geography consultant: Jeff Stanfield, Geography
   Inspector for Ofsted
Literacy consultant: Anne Spiring

All photographs were taken by Sue Cunningham.

Printed in China

Acknowledgements
The author would like to thank the following for their
help: the Cesaroni family; the principal, staff and pupils
of the Elementary School, Vaiano.

British Library Cataloguing in Publication Data
Tankard, Fiona
   Italy. – (Letters from around the world)
   1. Italy - Social conditions - 1994 - Juvenile literature
   2. Italy - Social life and customs - 1945 - Juvenile
   literature
   I. Title
   945'.093

ISBN 1842341707
13-digit ISBN (from 1 Jan 2007) 978 1 84234 170 4

Cover: Matteo and his football friends.
Title page: Matteo with his friends Marco, Lorenzo
   and Lucrezia.
This page: The *scuolabus* on its way to school.
Contents page: Matteo's grandad at work on his tractor.
Glossary page: Matteo's class and teacher.
Further information page: Matteo lights the bread oven.
Index: Matteo goes for a bike ride.

Contents

My Country

Monday, 7 January

Via Trasimeno 14
Poggi
06062 Castiglione del Lago
Italy

Dear Jo,

Ciao! (You say 'chow'. This means 'hi' or 'bye' in Italian.)

I'm Matteo Cesaroni and I'm 8 years old. I live in Poggi (you say 'podgy'), a small village in Umbria, central Italy. I have two sisters, Vanessa, who is 10 and Chiara, who is 5.

Being pen-friends will be great fun. Hurry up and write back soon!

From

Matteo

This is what I look like. Grandma, Dad, Vanessa, Mum, Chiara and Grandad are all on the balcony.

Italy lies in southern Europe, between the Mediterranean and Adriatic Seas.

Italy's place in the world.

SWITZERLAND
AUSTRIA
Monte Bianco
4,807m
A L P S
SLOVENIA
FRANCE
Lake Garda
Venice
Po
CROATIA
N
Adriatic Sea
Florence
Pisa
TUSCANY
Lake Trasimeno
Perugia
Poggi
Assisi
UMBRIA
Corsica
ITALY
Vatican City
ROME
Sardinia

0 50 100 150 200 kilometres
0   50   100 miles

Some people say that Italy looks like a boot kicking a ball. The country is divided into many regions. Umbria is one of them.

Sicily
Mediterranean Sea

Umbria is a quiet and beautiful region. One of its most famous towns is Assisi, where St Francis lived. Umbria is very popular with tourists.

Like much of Italy, there are many villages in Umbria. Many young people are now choosing to move to cities to find work.

Behind Matteo's house there are fields, olive trees and rows of vines.

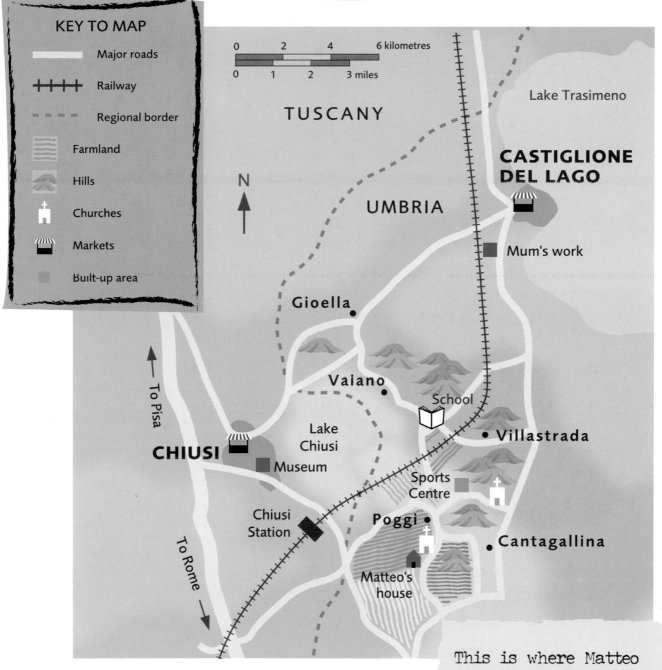

KEY TO MAP

- Major roads
- Railway
- Regional border
- Farmland
- Hills
- Churches
- Markets
- Built-up area

0   2   4   6 kilometres

0   1   2   3 miles

TUSCANY

UMBRIA

Lake Trasimeno

CASTIGLIONE DEL LAGO

Mum's work

N

Gioella

To Pisa

Vaiano

School

CHIUSI

Lake Chiusi

Museum

Villastrada

Sports Centre

Poggi

Cantagallina

Chiusi Station

To Rome

Matteo's house

This is where Matteo lives and goes to school.

Poggi means 'hills' in Italian and the village has lots of hills surrounding it.
The nearest big town is Chiusi, which is 7 kilometres away. Castiglione del Lago is another large town. It is 15 kilometres away. Matteo's family goes to the market there on Wednesdays.

Landscape and Weather

Umbria is a mountainous region. Its landscape is a patchwork of vineyards, olive groves, woods and fields. It also has the largest lake in central Italy, called Lake Trasimeno.

Grandad ploughs a field to make it ready for planting winter wheat.

The climate in northern Italy is cooler and wetter than in the south. Central Italy is hot in summer. In the winter it can be quite cold. Sometimes the mountains become covered in snow and people go there to ski.

Vanessa with olives
grown on the farm.
They are pressed
to make olive oil.

Umbria's Climate

January	July
Temperature	**Temperature**
5°C	25°C
76mm	43mm
Rainfall	**Rainfall**

At Home

Matteo's family lives in an old farmhouse. His grandparents live there, too. The original building is nearly 200 years old. As the Cesaroni family has grown, new rooms have been added to the building.

Long ago, cows used to live downstairs. The heat from their bodies kept the people upstairs warm.

This is the farmhouse.
Matteo lives downstairs.

Now the house has been turned into two apartments. Matteo's grandparents live in the one upstairs and Matteo's family lives on the ground floor.

Grandad and Matteo plant some garlic. Grandma uses garlic to flavour their food.

Matteo's family has three cats and three dogs. This is Chiara with her kitten, Stella.

Matteo adds wood to the bread oven.

Each apartment in the farmhouse has a kitchen, bathroom, living-room and three bedrooms. There is also a pantry, or *cantina*, to store the food that the family grows.

Not all homes in the area are like Matteo's. There are also modern houses and small apartment blocks.

Grandma in the *cantina* with her special tomato sauce.

Monday, 15 April

Via Trasimeno 14
Poggi
06062 Castiglione del Lago
Italy

Dear Jo,

It was great to get your letter last week. Did I tell you we've got a bread oven outside our house? My job is to gather bits of wood for it from around the farm. We use it for barbecues, or to cook Grandma's delicious pizzas.

Yesterday after lunch, Vanessa, Chiara and I played with our karaoke machine. It was great fun. I've got a good voice – well, I think so anyway!

Ciao,

Matteo

I love our karaoke machine, even though Vanessa says I sound like one of our cats!

Food and Mealtimes

On school days Matteo wakes up at 6.30 a.m.
For breakfast he has hot milk with a little coffee in
it and a *brioche*, a sweet cake. During the morning
he usually has a snack of fruit or sometimes
bruschetta, toasted bread with olive oil and garlic.

Grandma picks vegetables
from the garden.

Matteo buys fresh bread from Domenico, the bread man.

Vegetables for sale in the weekly market at Castiglione del Lago.

Matteo buys bread from the bread van, which comes to the house every day. Most of the family's vegetables are grown at home. The rest are bought from the local market.

Lunch is the main meal. It starts with pasta, maybe spaghetti or tagliatelle (flat spaghetti) with sauce. Next Matteo eats roast meat and vegetables. Afterwards he has fresh fruit from the orchard.

In the autumn, chestnuts are a special treat. Uncle Fabio is heating some for Chiara.

Sometimes Matteo's family has pizza for dinner.

Friday, 7 June

Via Trasimeno 14
Poggi
06062 Castiglione del Lago
Italy

Ciao Jo!

My grandma makes the best tagliatelle! Here's her recipe:

You will need: 300g plain flour, 1 litre of water,
3 large eggs, pinch of salt

1. Add the eggs and salt to the flour and mix with a fork.
2. Now mix everything together with your hands until it becomes a dough.
3. Knead the dough until it is smooth and stretchy. Leave it for 15 minutes to 'rest'.
4. Roll the dough out on a floured board until it is 2mm thick and cut it into 5mm-wide strips.
5. Cook the tagliatelle in 1 litre of boiling salted water for about 3–5 minutes.

It's delicious with hot tomato sauce! Try it and let me know if you like it.

From

Matteo

Grandma and I making tagliatelle.

School Day

Matteo goes to the primary school in Vaiano, a village 3 kilometres away. Most pupils travel to school by car or on the *scuolabus* (school bus). At about 7.15 a.m. Matteo catches the *scuolabus* outside his house.

Matteo's *scuolabus* picks up children from all the villages on the way to Vaiano.

This is Matteo's class in an English lesson.

School starts at 8 a.m. with assembly and finishes at 12.30 p.m. Twice a week, school finishes at 4.30 p.m. Matteo has lessons in maths, history, science, geography, religious studies, Italian and English.

Matteo's teacher, Paolo, helps him to use the computer.

Matteo has lunch in the school canteen.

In Italy, children start school at the age of 6. Matteo will stay at primary school until he is 11 years old. Then he will go to middle school. He will go to high school when he is 14.

After school Matteo and some of his friends play football.

Wednesday, 18 September

Via Trasimeno 14
Poggi
06062 Castiglione del Lago
Italy

Hi Jo,

I'm glad you liked the tagliatelle! At school today we played a game called 'Odds and Evens'. You should try it. Here's how to play:

1. Each player guesses 'odd' or 'even'.
2. Players shake their fists in time to this song:

    Let's throw them down
    At eleven o'clock –
    One, two, three...

3. On 'three' everyone holds out between zero and ten fingers. Add them up. The winner is the one who guessed 'odd' or 'even' correctly.

What do you do during break?
Write back and tell me.

Ciao,

Matteo

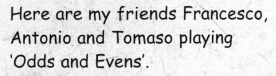

Here are my friends Francesco, Antonio and Tomaso playing 'Odds and Evens'.

Off to Work

Matteo's dad works for a building company. He delivers building materials all over the area in his lorry. Sometimes he has to drive very long distances.

Matteo's dad with his lorry.

Matteo's mum serves a customer at the supermarket check-out.

Matteo's mum works as a cashier at a supermarket in Castiglione del Lago. She is also in charge of ordering the food that the shop sells.

In Umbria many people are farmers. The area is also very popular with holiday-makers, so some people work in hotels and campsites.

A hotel receptionist welcomes a tourist to the area.

Free Time

There is always plenty to do on the farm. Matteo's dad spends much of his free time driving the tractor or repairing farm machinery.

Matteo helps his dad fix the tractor.

Matteo's favourite ride at the funfair is the dodgems.

When the farm work is done, Matteo's dad and Uncle Fabio sometimes go fishing on the lake. Matteo's mum likes to go to dancing classes with her friends.

The big, all-year funfair at Perugia is Matteo's favourite place to go at the weekends. He also enjoys riding his bike with friends.

The country roads around Poggi are fun and safe places for cycling.

Religion

Matteo's house has a small statue of the Madonna beside the window.

Most Italians are Roman Catholics, but Italy has several other religions, too.

Matteo's family is Roman Catholic. When Matteo is 10 years old, he will take lessons to prepare him for his First Communion.

Matteo's family visits the little church in Poggi.

Sunday, 3 November

Via Trasimeno 14
Poggi
06062 Castiglione del Lago
Italy

Dear Jo,

Yesterday it was the Day of the Dead. We took chrysanthemums to my great-grandma's grave in the cemetery at Villastrada. It's traditional here to visit our relatives' graves on this day or on 1 November, All Saints' Day.

Italy has lots of festivals. My favourite is *Ferragosto*, on 15 August, when everyone has a holiday and all the shops are closed. What's your favourite festival?

Ciao,

Matteo

Mum always puts flowers in the special flower holder for my great-grandma.

Fact File

Capital city: Rome is a very old city. There are many ancient buildings, including the Colosseum, where gladiators used to fight.

There is also a small independent state inside Rome, called Vatican City. This is where the Pope lives.

Other major cities: Florence, Venice and Pisa (home of the Leaning Tower of Pisa).

Neighbouring countries: France, Switzerland, Austria and Slovenia.

Size: 301,278 km²

Population: 57,784,000. This is quite similar to the UK.

Currency: The euro (€). This replaced the Italian lire in January 2002. There are 100 cents in a euro. It is now the currency used by twelve out of the fifteen members of the European Union.

It costs 0.41 euros to send a letter within Europe.

Flag: The Italian flag is based on the French flag, which has a blue stripe instead of a green one. This design was brought to Italy by Napoleon in 1797.

Languages: Italian is the official language. Some people also speak French, German and Slovene on the borders.

Main industries: Tourism, machinery, iron and steel, chemicals, cars, clothes, footwear and ceramics.

Longest river: The River Po, 652km. It is in the north of Italy.

Highest mountain: Mont Blanc (Monte Bianco in Italian), 4,807m. This is in the Alps in northern Italy.

Famous Italians:
Leonardo da Vinci painted the world's most famous painting, the *Mona Lisa*. He was born in Italy in 1452. He was an engineer, sculptor, painter and architect. Other famous Italians include Galileo Galilei, born in 1564, who among other things invented a type of telescope, and Guglielmo Marconi, born in 1874, who invented the radio.

Famous foods: Italy is most famous for foods such as ice-cream, pizza and pasta. There are over 300 kinds of pasta in Italy!

Main religions: Roman Catholicism is the main religion, but there is also Protestantism and Judaism. Catholic Italians celebrate Christmas and Easter. They have several other public holidays, including Epiphany on 6 January. This is also the day when Italian children expect a visit from the Epiphany witch, who brings presents if they have been good and leaves coal if they have been bad!

Glossary

All Saints' Day A Christian festival on 1 November to honour all the saints in the Christian Church.

brioche (You say 'bree-osh') A small, rounded sweet roll.

bruschetta (You say 'broo-sket-ta') Toasted bread with olive oil and garlic.

cantina A room where dried, tinned or bottled food is stored.

ciao (You say 'chow') This can mean 'hello' or 'bye'.

Colosseum A big, circular building in Rome with seats all round an arena. It was built between AD75 and AD80.

Day of the Dead A special prayer day on 2 November when people pray for the dead.

Epiphany This is the celebration of the coming of the three wise men after Jesus was born. It is always on 6 January.

European Union A group of 15 countries in Europe that work and trade together.

First Communion The time when a young person can take a full part in the Catholic church service and receive the holy bread and wine.

gladiators Men who were trained to fight in arenas to entertain people in ancient Roman times.

karaoke machine A machine that plays the tunes of popular songs, while you sing the words.

Madonna Another name for the Virgin Mary.

Pope The head of the Roman Catholic Church.

state An area within a country that is like a 'mini-country'.

tagliatelle (You say 'tal-ya-tel-leh') Tagliatelle is pasta shaped in long, thin strips.

Further Information

Information books:

A Flavour of Italy by Saviour Pirotta (Hodder Wayland, 1999)

Italy by Miles Harvey (Children's Press, 1998)

Next Stop: Italy by Fred Martin (Heinemann Library, 1998)

Picture a Country: Italy by Henry Pluckrose (Franklin Watts, 1998)

Fiction:

Biancabella and Other Italian Fairy Tales ed. Annie MacDonell et al. (Dover Publications, 2001)

The Orphan Singer by Emily Arnold McCully (Arthur A. Levine Books, 2001)

We're on our way to Italy by Haydn Middleton (Scholastic, 2000)

Resource packs:

The Wallace Collection Italian Renaissance Individual Resource Pack The Wallace Collection Mail Order, Hertford House, Manchester Square, London WIM 6BN. Schools Liaison Officer, Tel: 020 7563 9651

Websites:

CIA World Factbook
www.cia.gov/cia/publications/factbook/
Basic facts and figures about Italy and other countries.

In Italy Online
www.initaly.com/
General travel information about Italy.

Giardino Italiano.
http://www.giardino.it/junior/
Website made by children for children around the world, with links to Italian pen-friends.

Index